Original title:
Guffaws Among the Grass

Copyright © 2025 Creative Arts Management OÜ
All rights reserved.

Author: Matthew Whitaker
ISBN HARDBACK: 978-1-80567-336-1
ISBN PAPERBACK: 978-1-80567-635-5

Mirthful Memories in the Open Air

In fields where laughter dances free,
Chasing butterflies as we agree,
With each stumble, a giggle spills,
Joyful echoes that nature drills.

We roll like tumbleweeds in sun,
Tickling toes, oh what fun!
A frog hops by with quite a leap,
We share a chuckle, laughter deep.

Clouds parade, the sky's a stage,
Every joke, a never-ending page.
With grass as cushions, we lay back,
In stitches now, lost in our track.

As twilight falls, the fireflies gleam,
Chasing shadows like a comic dream.
With smiles wide, our hearts take flight,
In memories made, the joy feels right.

Glee Amidst the Growing

In the meadow where daisies sway,
A rabbit hops in a comical way.
The squirrel chases its own fluffy tail,
While butterflies dance, setting the sail.

A frog croaks jokes from his lily pad,
While nearby, the ladybug looks quite glad.
With giggles echoing up to the sky,
Nature's laughter makes moments fly.

Elevated Spirits in the Grassy Haven

Beneath the arch of the sun's warm light,
A picnic spreads, everything's just right.
Ants form a line, as if on parade,
Marshmallows roast, and memories made.

The wind carries whispers of jests untold,
While flowers bloom, bright in colors bold.
Nearby, a puppy chases its own shoe,
In this grassy haven, joy feels brand new.

Harmonious Whispers from Nature

The crickets chirp in a playful tune,
As shadows stretch to greet the moon.
Even the breeze seems to giggle and sway,
With secrets lost in the twilight play.

Fireflies flicker in games of delight,
Painting the dark with their luminous light.
A dance of delight in the cool evening's breath,
Where laughter lingers, defying death.

Melody of Joy in the Garden

In the garden where colors collide,
A sunflower grins, swollen with pride.
Grasshoppers jump in a rhythmic flurry,
Creating a song, no hint of worry.

Bees hum sweetly, a buzzing brigade,
Fluttering petals begin their parade.
Every bloom seems to sparkle and shine,
In this joyful place, where all hearts align.

Joyous Journeys Around the Plants

Bouncing bugs in silly hats,
Chasing bees with playful chats,
Flowers giggle, petals wink,
Nature's laughter makes us think.

Frogs croak jokes by lily pads,
While sneaky snails play tricks on lads,
Insects dance in a twinkling line,
Echoing giggles sweet as wine.

Wiggly worms in party shoes,
Spin around like they can't lose,
Sunshine sprinkles laughter bright,
As shadows play and leap with light.

Dancing leaves make music swell,
Each rustle tells a funny tale,
Joyful roots in the soil alight,
In this verdant, merry site.

Whirl of Whimsy in the Breeze

Breezy whispers tickle trees,
As they sway with the carefree tease,
Clouds in costumes drift and sway,
Tickling thoughts in a breezy play.

Squirrels chase their mischievous dreams,
While sunlight spills like flowing streams,
The wind chuckles, swirls around,
In the echoes where joy is found.

Ticklish grass beneath our toes,
Sprouts of laughter where humor grows,
Each moment spun from light and glee,
Crickets hum in harmony.

Through this whirl of fun, we dance,
In nature's arms, we take a chance,
Joyful heartbeats, playful cheer,
A tapestry of laughter here.

Serenity in the Shimmering Fields

In shimmering meadows, laughter flows,
With daisies peeking, oh how it glows,
Butterflies flutter with whimsy bright,
Turning the calm into pure delight.

Grasshoppers leap with comic grace,
As shadows play a merry chase,
The breeze brings giggles from afar,
Even the moon peeks in to spar.

Swaying stalks in playful jest,
Collude with clouds, who're never pressed,
In every rustling wave, we find,
A gentle laugh, a tranquil mind.

Serene laughter wraps the land,
In nature's arms, we make our stand,
Together sharing this gift so sweet,
Where freedom laughs beneath our feet.

Cheerful Tributes to Nature's Canvas

Canvas bright with splashes bold,
Each hue a giggle, tales retold,
Nature's brush strokes tickle air,
As petals flaunt their charm with flair.

Beetles parade in shiny coats,
While minnows mimic fancy boats,
In this gallery of cheer,
Every corner sings, and we're drawn near.

Whimsical scenes where laughter grows,
Hi-fives of raindrops, goodness flows,
Sun-kissed edges, colors beam,
Painting joy in a brilliant dream.

Nature chuckles, smiles widely here,
In every nook, we feel the cheer,
With whispers of love that softly chant,
Life's joyful art, in nature's grant.

Flash of Fun in the Foliage

In the shade where shadows play,
A squirrel winks, then bounds away.
A tickle breeze through leafy throngs,
Whispers secrets, sings along.

Bunnies hop with giggling sounds,
Chasing bugs that dance around.
The sunbeams dance like jolly sprites,
Lighting up their playful flights.

A butterfly with colors bright,
Swings and swirls, a dizzy sight.
The flowers chuckle, petals tease,
As laughter mingles with the breeze.

Mirth on the Meadow's Edge

Here the daisies twist and sway,
As fluffy clouds drift on their way.
Grasshoppers leap in joyful play,
While sunshine showers warm the day.

A piglet rolls, a muddy mound,
Its oinks a chorus, all around.
The robin sings with glee in flight,
A cheerful tune to greet the light.

Children tumble, shout, and cheer,
With giggles ringing loud and clear.
Nature's laughter fills the air,
In every nook, it's everywhere.

Chimes in the Canopy

Above the green, the branches sway,
A raccoon chuckles in the fray.
The leaves all whisper, secrets to
The wind that dances on cue.

An owl glances, eyes so wide,
Its silly hoot can't be denied.
As squirrels race, they trip and fall,
Each tumble echoes, laughter's call.

The sunbeams filter through the trees,
To tickle down the bumblebees.
They buzz and dance, a merry throng,
In this bright world, we all belong.

Rejuvenation Through Laughter

In the meadow, where joy starts,
The daisies play their little parts.
With every breeze that tickles by,
The butterflies begin to fly.

A puppy bounds with floppy ears,
Creating laughter, calming fears.
With every bark, a giggle springs,
In cheerful symphony, all sing.

The green grass waves, a funny sight,
As shadows dance in fading light.
With every smile, the world feels bright,
Laughter lifts us to new heights.

Blooming Banter

In the garden, laughter swells,
Petals giggle, secrets tell.
Bumblebees with buzzing cheer,
Dance around without a fear.

Sunlight drapes on every hue,
Flowers chat with morning dew.
Their voices blend in bright array,
As joy unfolds in sunny play.

Roots and stems in playful fight,
Tickling each with pure delight.
The breeze joins in, a lively friend,
Where silly tales will never end.

Amidst the blooms, tales roam free,
Whispering joy in harmony.
Nature's jesters, bold and bright,
Painting days with purest light.

Revelry of the Rustling Leaves

Leaves giggle in the playful breeze,
Whirling whispers dance with ease.
They twirl and twist in joyous song,
Nature's laughter, vibrant, strong.

Tree trunks chuckle, roots entwined,
In every creak, a joke well-timed.
Squirrels leap with funny flair,
Adding mischief to the air.

Branches sway as if they jest,
Knocking acorns, never rest.
The sun shines down, a radiant smile,
Amidst the fun, let's stay awhile.

Rustling leaves, a merry crew,
Inviting all to join the view.
With every rustle, joy attaches,
Laughter echoes, nature matches.

Jests Under the Open Sky

Beneath the wide and playful sky,
Clouds drift slow, as if to pry.
With every shape, they spark a grin,
A race begins, let's join the spin.

The sun reveals its cheeky glow,
Warming hearts, making smiles grow.
Birds chirp jokes in feathered glee,
Singing tales from tree to tree.

Laughter rides on playful winds,
Pulling at our skin like friends.
Every breeze, a nudge of fun,
Under the antics of the sun.

With splashes of bright hues above,
The world wraps tight in threads of love.
Jests abound, sweet and spry,
Under the humor of the open sky.

Harmony of Happiness

In fields where giggles softly blend,
Colors and laughter twist and wend.
Every flower, a little joke,
With petals dancing, spirits stoke.

Birds chirp tunes of pure delight,
Join the fun from dawn till night.
Butterflies flutter with a wink,
In this world, we pause to think.

Sunbeams tickle grass below,
As shadows play and embers glow.
Life's a fest, a merry ring,
Where hearts unite, and laughs take wing.

Harmony flows in every laugh,
Nature's own playful epitaph.
With open arms, we rise and cheer,
For happiness is always near.

Elation Under the Skies

Laughter bubbles, shrubs dance along,
A squirrel in a tie sings a silly song.
Butterflies giggle, butterflies glide,
While daisies create a merry slide.

Tickles of sunlight, hugs from the breeze,
A picnic of whimsy beneath swaying trees.
A bird with a hat hops by with a grin,
Welcoming joy where the fun begins.

Friends with big smiles, spread laughter around,
Chasing the shadows that frolic on ground.
Bubbles of wishes float high in the air,
While everyone dances without a care.

With each tiny giggle, the world spins with glee,
A realm full of chuckles, wild and free.
Playful and vibrant, like colors in art,
Elation paints scenes straight from the heart.

Blissful Babble in Bloom

Petals are chatting, in colors so bright,
They whisper funny tales, oh what a sight!
Bees buzz with laughter, a comical tune,
As flowers all sway beneath the full moon.

A rabbit in glasses is reading a book,
The buzz of the blooms, oh, take a good look!
While daisies play peek-a-boo, shadows disguise,
In harmony, giggles arise to the skies.

A breeze that is ticklish, rustles the leaves,
As crickets share secrets no one believes.
Sunshine wraps warmly around bustling buds,
Creating a symphony of beautiful thuds.

Buds burst with mirth at the slapstick parade,
Wondrous and witty, brilliantly laid.
In moments of sunshine, all worries just fade,
A landscape of laughter in nature's charade.

Radiant Moments in the Greenery

Dancing shadows twirl, like joy in a spin,
Grass tickles toes, and laughter comes in.
A hedgehog in shoes, what a peculiar sight,
Rolls down a hill, pure delight in the light!

Each leaf holds a giggle, each bark has a jest,
Frogs croak in rhythm, they do their best.
Nature's loud laughter fills up the day,
Echoes of joy playfully sway.

With every green patch comes a burst of glee,
Wondrous convulsions of humor in spree.
The sun casts a grin on the vibrant terrain,
While ants march along in a whimsical train.

Moments of mirth in the thick leafy maze,
Life dances sweetly, in unpredictable ways.
With each little chuckle, the world seems to cheer,
Together in fun, there's nothing to fear.

Bright Faces in the Landscape

In fields where the daisies do sway and do bend,
Bright faces chuckle, it seems never to end.
A cow wearing sunglasses lounges with flair,
While bunnies in bow ties hop without care.

Laughter erupts like a fountain of joy,
As colorful creatures frolic and toy,
Whimsy is painted on each playful smirk,
In fields of enchantment, where giggles lurk.

The sunbeams are grinning, reflecting the fun,
A parade of bright pigments under the sun.
With butterflies swooping for a dance in the light,
Every moment is magic, every laugh feels so bright.

Under the arches of big, leafy boughs,
Life's chuckles abound, from here to the cows.
In a landscape of laughter, we all find our place,
Together we revel, with joy we embrace.

Laughter Whispered in the Meadow

In fields where daisies dance with delight,
The bumblebees buzz with all of their might.
Butterflies giggle, flitting around,
While sunbeams tickle the soft, verdant ground.

A rabbit prances, playing his part,
Chasing his shadow, quick and smart.
Laughter spills over like a bubbling stream,
In a world of whimsy, a delightful dream.

Giggles Beneath the Willow

Beneath the branches where whispers play,
A squirrel cracks jokes in a cheeky way.
The old willow chuckles, swaying with grace,
As friends share stories, smiles on each face.

The frogs join in with a ribbiting cheer,
Creating a symphony that's perfectly clear.
With every leap and every small pounce,
The joy of the moment makes laughter bounce.

Chuckles in the Wildflowers

In a patch of colors, vibrant and bright,
The petals are giggling, what a sweet sight!
A ladybug teeters, playful and spry,
Spreading chuckles under the vast, sunny sky.

With a touch of whimsy, the grass starts to sway,
As children run wild, gleeful at play.
Each rustling leaf sings a tune full of cheer,
Beneath the blue skies where smiles disappear.

Joyful Echoes of the Field

The wind carries laughter, so light and so free,
It dances with echoes, a sweet jubilee.
Cattle low softly as they munch on the grass,
While funny old crickets come out to amass.

In every corner, delight fills the air,
With stories of antics so wonderfully rare.
The sun sets in splendor, a canvas of fun,
As laughter rings out, the day's almost done.

Swaying with Mischief

In the meadow where pranks unfold,
A chicken danced, so bold and cold.
Bouncing on toes, it stole the show,
With feathers fluffed, it put on a glow.

A squirrel played tricks on a dainty snail,
Tickling its shell, a comical tale.
Laughter erupted, the flowers shook,
As nature's jesters put on their look.

With ants in bow ties and bugs in a band,
The grass cheered loudly, they didn't quite stand.
A parade of giggles swept through the scene,
As sunlight painted a vibrant sheen.

So here's to the laughter, the joy in the air,
In this lively place, without a single care.
Mischief and mirth spin 'round like a dance,
In the heart of the meadow, where all take the chance.

Amusement Among the Blossoms

Daisy and rose had a playful spat,
While tulips chuckled, imagine that!
The wind shared jokes with the bumblebee,
As petals waggled in pure jubilee.

The sun's warm grin lit up every face,
While shadows beneath began a merry race.
Busy bees buzzed, doing the cha-cha,
While ladybugs laughed at the old tarantula.

Jasmine sang low, a silly old tune,
While daisies swayed to the rhythm of noon.
All around, nature's jests piled high,
As butterflies chuckled, drifting on by.

In gardens of mirth where smiles come alive,
Every blossom joins in, oh how they thrive!
With blooms full of giggles, and scents of delight,
The stage is set, in colors so bright.

Cheers from the Nature's Stage

A rabbit recited a joke quite absurd,
While crickets chimed in with chirps that were heard.
The sun waved its arms, a stellar embrace,
As laughter erupted from every small space.

The brook babbled soft with a tickle and cheer,
While frogs played a tune, they held very dear.
With splashes and hops in a raucous song,
The audience echoed where they all belong.

The trees clapped their branches, a rustling sound,
As squirrels performed their antics profound.
Roses bloomed wide, guarding the scene,
In this comedic play, there's much to glean.

In this theater wild, under skies so blue,
Each giggle and chuckle brought dreams anew.
We'll linger a while, let the fun never stop,
With winks to the clouds, on this joyful rooftop.

Lighthearted Lyrics of the Land

In fields where laughter shines like the sun,
The grass tells tales of all kinds of fun.
A puppy rolled over, chasing a bee,
As daisies giggled, 'Come dance with me!'

The crow cracked a pun, unmatched by the rest,
While clouds held their breath, it was all just the best.
With shadows that leaped through the golden glow,
The earth offered up joyful acts in a show.

Ants conga-lined, in their tiny parade,
Each step brought a smile, a moment well-made.
The warmth of the breeze whispered secrets so sweet,
In this joyful land, where laughter's replete.

With tunes from the grass and the rustle of trees,
Every heart found a beat, carried on by the breeze.
So come join the fun, in this land we adore,
Where lighthearted lyrics make spirits soar.

Chimes of Laughter in the Glen

In the glen where giggles bloom,
A ticklish breeze begins to zoom,
Wobbling critters dance with glee,
Found in this mirthful jubilee.

With every hop and silly shout,
Friends tumble down, a playful bout,
Laughter echoes through the trees,
A symphony of light, sweet tease.

The sunbeams play, they twist and turn,
While cheeky rabbits dare to learn,
Who can jump the highest today?
In this glen, we laugh and play.

So come and join this merry throng,
Where every heart knows it belongs,
In joyful dance, we freely spin,
A chime of laughter to begin.

Escapades Beneath the Skies

Under vast and chortling skies,
Adventures spark like fireflies,
With every twist and silly chase,
We carve out joy in every space.

The clouds, they giggle as they drift,
While friends bestow their funny gift,
A pratfall here, a stumble there,
Laughter floats upon the air.

In the meadows, we play pretend,
As laughter trails around the bend,
With every smile, a new surprise,
Escapades beneath these skies.

Through fields where whimsical winds whirl,
As daisies dance, we jump and twirl,
With hearts alight, our spirits soar,
In joyous bonds, forevermore.

Frivolous Capering in the Open Fields

In open fields where clowns convene,
They juggle joy, a sight serene,
With every tumble, giggles burst,
In frivolous capers, we quench our thirst.

The daisies nod, they know our game,
As garden gnomes cheer us, proclaim,
A wobbly dance, a cheerful cheer,
In this joyful place, there's nothing to fear.

Kites take flight on breezy trails,
Waving at us with laughter's sails,
We chase our dreams with funny flair,
Laughter bubbles in the open air.

Beneath the sun-drenched skies so bright,
Every moment feels just right,
Our hearts leap high, our smiles yield,
In joyful chaos of this field.

Tickles in the Treetops

In the treetops, whispers play,
Where silly squirrels frolic and sway,
With every leap, a chuckle flies,
Tickles echo through the skies.

Branches shake with playful glee,
As birds compose a symphony,
Each note a giggle, light and free,
In treetop realms of jubilee.

The wind it dances, soft and sly,
Painting laughter as it glides by,
With acrobatics high and wild,
Every moment keeps us riled.

So let us climb, let spirits soar,
With tickles calling wanting more,
In this playground above the ground,
Where every giggle can be found.

Whimsical Whispers of Joy

Laughter dances on the breeze,
Tickling toes and swaying trees.
A squirrel dons a tiny hat,
While crickets play their tunes sleek and fat.

Clouds are kites in the blue above,
Painting skies with strokes of love.
Each flower winks with a secret glee,
Inviting all, come play with me!

Jumpy puppies roam the glen,
Chasing shadows again and again.
A butterfly flutters with delicate grace,
Leading each grin to a jovial face.

Underneath the sun's warm embrace,
Nature's stage hosts a whimsical race.
Every giggle and every cheer,
Echoes sweetly from far and near.

Sunshine and Smiles in the Meadow

Bumbles buzz with a joyful flair,
While daisies dance with no care.
A rabbit hops, wearing a bow,
Chasing its tail in a merry show.

The brook tickles stones with a giggle,
While frogs leap and wiggle.
Each rustle hints at playful schemes,
In the land where laughter beams.

Sunbeams bounce on children's heads,
As they tumble down from their beds.
A kite zigzags the sky so bright,
Drawing laughter into the light.

Even the bees, with their buzzing hum,
Join the fun, making hearts go thrum.
In a patch where smiles freely flow,
Every moment starts to glow.

Nature's Festive Revel

The trees wear crowns of leafy blooms,
While laughter erupts from hidden rooms.
A badger prances with prideful grace,
As butterflies flitter in a colorful chase.

From hedges green, a chorus sings,
Harmonies of life, oh, the joy it brings!
Woodpeckers drum a merry beat,
Celebrating all with their rhythmic feet.

The sun spills gold on the waving wheat,
While little feet pace a playful beat.
A piglet twirls in the soft, warm mud,
Creating splashes while others thud.

Picnics spread with a whimsical flair,
Cookies, berries, and giggles to share.
Nature's revel, joyful and bright,
Fills the heart with pure delight.

Blissful Tumult of the Trodden Trail

On the trail where footsteps play,
Joyful whispers lead the way.
Laughter echoed off each stone,
As friends roamed, never alone.

A raccoon sports a look so sly,
With twinkling eyes that can't lie.
Each bend reveals a goofy sight,
Giggling shadows in the fading light.

The wind carries tales of delight,
Of mischief woven through the night.
Bouncing along, we skip with glee,
Chasing shadows, wild and free.

Nature's comedy, a rollicking show,
Each step ignites a new hello.
In the blissful muddle, let joy prevail,
On this cheerful, trodden trail.

Silly Serenades of the Garden

In the garden, ducks parade,
With funny hats, they serenade.
A cat in boots starts to prance,
While worms join in the merry dance.

Bumblebees with tiny drums,
Buzzing beats the rhythm hums.
Flowers giggle, petals sway,
Chasing clouds on a bright day.

A squirrel swings from leafy hinges,
Telling jokes while he cringes.
The sun above winks with glee,
As laughter rolls like waves at sea.

Among the blooms, joy's refrain,
Every giggle, every gain.
In this place where fun holds sway,
Nature's jesters steal the day.

Merriment in the Meadow Beads

In the meadow, hop and skip,
A rabbit makes a cheeky quip.
Ladybugs in twos and threes,
Waltzing on the gentle breeze.

Butterflies in colors bright,
Laugh as they take flight, so light.
Grasshoppers tickle soft and low,
Their banter puts on quite a show.

The sunbeams filter through the leaves,
While blushing petals share their thieves.
Every shadow tells a tale,
Of giggles that will never pale.

Swaying grasses join the fun,
Underneath the golden sun.
In this meadow full of cheer,
Every chuckle, oh so near.

Grins Beneath the Cedar Canopy

Underneath the cedar vine,
A raccoon sips on mixed brine.
With twinkling eyes and clumsy feet,
He juggles nuts, oh what a treat!

A frog leaps high, a funny croak,
As nearby squirrels share a joke.
The breeze is filled with laughter loud,
While shadows dance beneath the shroud.

The soil hums a cheerful tune,
As daisies twirl beneath the moon.
In this haven, joy is spry,
Every grin reaches for the sky.

Under branches, smiles bloom,
Chasing all away the gloom.
Nature's jesters, wild and free,
Beneath the trees, sheer jubilee.

Playful Shadows on the Grass

Shadows play tag on sun-kissed leaves,
As a wise old owl grins and heaves.
A chipmunk slides in a grassy race,
Winking at all in this merry space.

Near the pond, frogs leap with flair,
Singing choruses without a care.
The clouds drift by, styles on display,
Each puff a hat for fun's ballet.

The breeze tickles with whispers of joy,
Even the daisies wink, oh boy!
Every rustle and gentle sway,
Adds laughter to the sunlit day.

With each shadow's playful prance,
Together all, we laugh and dance.
In this land of gleeful sights,
The world shines with silly delights.

Joyous Rustle of the Blades

In fields where laughter flows,
The whispers dance and tease,
Tiny ants in bowler hats,
Prance with utmost ease.

Breezes tickle flowers bright,
They sway and bend with grace,
A rabbit hops, a jester's role,
In this delightful place.

The sunbeams share a joke or two,
With clouds that float so high,
While butterflies in costumes play,
Beneath the laughter sky.

Crickets chirp their silly tunes,
As shadows start to stretch,
In nature's merry, lively jest,
Joy is quite the fetch.

Frolicsome Fun by the Riverrun.

Where waters giggle, splash and swirl,
The pebbles laugh along,
Frogs croon their comical songs,
As dragonflies move strong.

A squirrel juggles acorns bright,
With antics just for fun,
Bouncing here, then over there,
Under the warm sun.

With each ripple sings a tale,
Of antics wild and free,
A dance upon the river's edge,
Brings smiles to you and me.

The willows share a secret or two,
In whispers soft and low,
As we all join the cheerful jest,
Where laughter loves to flow.

Laughter in the Meadow

Sun-kissed fields where giggles bloom,
And daisies join the cheer,
A snaggle-toothed grin from a little pup,
Chasing butterflies near.

Hares in silly hop-along,
Compete for best in show,
Each jump a comedic delight,
Stealing the lively glow.

A painted lady flits about,
In playful swirls of flight,
While bees break out in buzzing jokes,
In the soft, golden light.

The breeze carries hearty chuckles,
From the orchard to the vale,
Where joy hangs thick like morning mist,
On this playful trail.

Whispers of Cheer and Sun

The daisies gossip 'neath the rays,
In the dappled garden's grace,
While sunbeams tickle petals soft,
With a warm and bright embrace.

A hedgehog dons a silly hat,
And dances with the breeze,
While ladybugs throw tiny balls,
In midair, with such ease.

The grasshoppers tell knock-knock jokes,
With every joyful jump,
As butterflies in silly bands,
Gather 'round for a lump.

So let us share this radiant joy,
As laughter takes its flight,
In whispers soft, beneath the sun,
Our hearts are truly light.

Mirth in the Tall Blades

In fields where laughter takes its flight,
A squirrel juggles nuts, what a sight!
The daisies giggle, swaying with glee,
As butterflies dance, wild and free.

A frog leaps high, lands with a splat,
The crickets chirp, 'What was that?'
A rabbit grins, with a twitching nose,
As the sun dips low, the fun just grows.

With every rustle and playful tease,
The tall blades whisper, carried by a breeze.
Nature's jesters in vibrant array,
Sharing secrets at the close of day.

So come join the jest, let laughter reign,
In the patchwork quilt of our grassy plain.
Where joy is found in simple delight,
And every moment sparkles so bright.

Snickers at Sunset

As the sun sets low, the whispers begin,
A cat in a hat dreams of fishy din.
The owls roll their eyes, in soft twilight,
While foxes tell tales, their eyes all bright.

The gophers dig deep, a comical spree,
With each clumsy tumble, their giggles run free.
Fireflies flicker, like stars on a string,
Dancing in circles, joy on the wing.

As shadows grow long, the humor expands,
A raccoon plots mischief with clever hands.
With nature's chuckle wrapped in the air,
Each chuckle resounds, no worry or care.

So gather 'round as the day bids adieu,
In a meadow alive, where laughter is true.
With cada laugh, a spark ignites the night,
In this world of whimsy, all feels so right.

Hilarity in the Hills

On hills where chuckles roll down like streams,
A troupe of sheep play out their wild dreams.
With woolly hats and a boisterous shout,
They prance and they hop, all worries cast out.

The daisies peek in, with cheeks all aglow,
As a goat butts in, causing laughter to flow.
A jolly old postman trips on a log,
With parcels that tumble, covered in fog.

From the top of the hill, they share a delight,
With squirrelly antics and jokes out of sight.
The sun's last rays drape like ribbons of gold,
While the giggles of youth return tales of old.

So here in the hills, where joy takes a stand,
Every step brings laughter, a whimsical band.
Join in the frolic, let loose and be free,
In this merry land, where all smile with glee.

Chortles from the Evergreen

In the shelter of trees where the wild things play,
A chipmunk recounts the funniest day.
With a twitch of its tail, it spins a great tale,
While feathers of bluebirds add to the scale.

The pine needles rustle, like laughter in flight,
As the boughs sway gently in sheer delight.
A squirrel with acorns dons a grand crown,
Declaring a party, to never frown.

Giggling streams snake through mossy green beds,
Tickling the ferns, raising mirth from their heads.
A wise old owl blinks, can't help but join in,
With a hoot of approval, let the fun begin!

So gather the friends from the thicket and glade,
Where echoes of mirth are forever displayed.
In this evergreen haven, let joy take its leave,
For laughter and whimsy are all we believe.

Gleeful Gatherings of the Untamed

In fields where daisies sway and dance,
The critters join in a merry prance.
A squirrel dons a hat too wide,
While rabbits giggle, side by side.

A chicken clucks a silly tune,
As fireflies twirl beneath the moon.
With every hop and every squawk,
The forest echoes with their talk.

A bear plays tag with a sneaky fox,
Crafted tricks within the rocks.
The shadows shift in playful cheer,
Laughter rings, it's plain and clear.

So gather round, let spirits lift,
In nature's world, we share this gift.
With joyous hearts and silly ways,
We celebrate these sunlit days.

Enchanted Laughter in the Wilderness

A rabbit tells a tale so bold,
Of escapades in fields of gold.
While owls chuckle in the trees,
Their hoots a dance upon the breeze.

A goat in specs plays wisdom's role,
She shares her thoughts, a wise old soul.
The chipmunks chime in as they debate,
On who will win the race, what fate!

Beneath the stars, on soft green beds,
They spin their stories, weave their threads.
From blissful dreams to giggles shared,
In every heart, joy is declared.

The night is young, let laughter reign,
Through every jest, we break the chain.
In this wild land, we seek the light,
With merry souls, we dance till night.

Whirlwinds of Wit and Wonder

A gust of wind, a hat takes flight,
It sails away, what a funny sight!
The ducks are quacking, flapping wide,
As tiny turtles peek with pride.

The frogs recite their playful rhymes,
Each leap a chuckle, lost in times.
Amongst the blooms, a jest unfolds,
With every bloom, a secret told.

A dancing twig and jiggly leaf,
Bring giggles forth, dissolve all grief.
With every twirl, the world is bright,
Our hearts unite, creating light.

So let the whims of laughter soar,
In wildest ways, we crave for more.
With every grin, and each small cheer,
This joyful land is calling near.

Trills of Joy in the Tall Grass

In meadows deep, where shadows play,
Grasshoppers skip in bright array.
A peacock struts with feathers wide,
While crickets chirp, and friends abide.

A silly goat with a fluffy beard,
Tells jokes so grand, it's truly weird.
The flowers sway, they join the fun,
As laughter spreads beneath the sun.

With every rustle, mysteries tease,
As butterflies dance upon the breeze.
The world's a stage where joy takes flight,
In every heart, the spark ignites.

So come and join this merry spree,
Among the grass, we all are free.
With smiles and grins, we weave a tale,
In this great expanse, we shall not fail.

Joyful Serenade of Nature

In the meadow where rabbits race,
Chasing whispers in a peaceful space.
Flowers giggle, swaying with delight,
The sun winks down, a warm, golden sight.

A butterfly flutters, painting the air,
While ants in a line march without a care.
Squirrels chatter, plotting their next scheme,
Nature's laughter flows like a bubbling stream.

Leaves rustle softly, tickling the breeze,
As frogs croak jokes from their cozy trees.
The breeze carries chuckles, light and spry,
In this joyful haven, the spirits fly.

With every rustle, a giggle is found,
Life dances lightly on this playful ground.
In nature's embrace, joy finds its way,
As smiles bloom bright under the sun's ray.

Tickles in the Thicket

In the thicket deep, where shadows play,
The brambles hum tunes that frolic and sway.
A fox with a grin prances by with flair,
Tickling the hedgehog without a care.

The owls share secrets, whooing with glee,
As squirrels jive on their branches free.
Bumblebees buzz in a humorous twist,
Creating laughter that can't be missed.

Ducks quack out rhythms, a silly parade,
While wildflowers dance in colorful spade.
The sun peeks through with a chuckle so bright,
Illuminating joy in the soft, green light.

With every rustle, the excitement grows,
Nature sings merrily, in rhythms it flows.
In the thicket wild, with all things alive,
The heart finds a place where giggles thrive.

Jubilant Journey Through the Green

A stroll through the grove ignites the smiles,
   Where cheerful breezes glide for miles.
   The daisies dance in a hopping spree,
      Waving hello to the busy bee.

The brook babbles jokes as it tumbles around,
   While critters unite in a symphonic sound.
   Laughter leaps from each rustling bush,
   Tickling the leaves in a jubilant hush.

   The towering trees share stories so bold,
Of adventures and secrets that never grow old.
   Amidst the tall grass, a fox takes a dip,
   Chasing the echoes of a whimsical quip.

   On this joyous journey, every step sings,
With heartwarming laughter that nature brings.
   So under the sky, where the wild things are,
Every smile shines brighter than a twinkling star.

Chortles in the Orchard

In the orchard lush, the branches play tricks,
With laughing leaves and their nimble flicks.
The apples giggle, hanging low and bright,
As the wind carries jokes through the sun's light.

Birds perched above sing a raucous tune,
Tickling the air with a cheerful swoon.
The rabbits hop high, in a race so grand,
With playful antics all perfectly planned.

Beneath the boughs, joy loudly blooms,
As bees buzz around in their busy rooms.
With every bump, a chuckle unfolds,
In nature's delight, where brightness beholds.

In this merry orchard, laughter runs free,
Creating a symphony of pure jubilee.
With each joyful sound that dances in the air,
Nature spreads humor beyond compare.

Giggles Beneath the Trees

Underneath the leafy boughs,
Squirrels dance in silly rows.
Branches swaying, full of cheer,
Whispers echo, laughter near.

Sunlight dapples, shadows play,
Bouncing blooms in bright display.
Here, the world has lost its cares,
Joyful hearts float through the air.

Rabbits hop in fancy shoes,
Munching clover, sharing views.
Every rustle brings delight,
Nature's stage, a funny sight.

With each breeze, a giggle flows,
Tickling leaves, where fun just grows.
Beneath the trees, our spirits soar,
Finding laughter, evermore.

Joyful Echoes in the Fields

Fields of green, a playful scene,
Dancing daisies, bright and keen.
Bees do buzz, and butterflies,
Twist and twirl 'neath sunny skies.

Total chaos—oh my word!
Chickens chase a startled bird.
Birthday clouds in skies of blue,
Playful pranks in all we do.

Lively laughter fills the air,
Bouncing joy is everywhere.
In this space of pure delight,
Every moment feels just right.

Count the giggles, one by one,
Underneath the warming sun.
Joyful echoes fill the fields,
Here, our happiness unveils.

Chuckles in the Wildflowers

In wildflower patches, blooms abound,
Laughter ripples through the ground.
Bumblebees with hums and dives,
Joyful antics, nature thrives.

Petals giggle in the breeze,
Whisper secrets through the trees.
Dandelions cheerfully sway,
Making wishes, come what may.

Frogs in ponds share silly jokes,
While curious ducks, in quacks, invoke.
Every moment, pure delight,
A symphony of giggles bright.

When the sun begins to set,
Chasing shadows, never fret.
In wildflowers, the chuckles grow,
Painting joy in every show.

Mirth Among the Ferns

Ferns stand tall, with wisdom grand,
Whisper stories from the land.
They unlock the funny lore,
Riddles echo through the floor.

Little critters scurry fast,
Creating moments that won't last.
A playful tap, a joyful slide,
Nature's laughter cannot hide.

Beneath the folds, the giggles bloom,
Fragrant earth dispels all gloom.
Every rustle, every cheer,
Inviting all to gather near.

With each breeze, the mirth goes round,
In every corner, joy is found.
Among the ferns, life's dance unfolds,
In laughter's warmth, each heart beholds.

Jests in the Sunlit Glade

In the glade where shadows play,
Tiny sprites come out to sway.
With a wink and playful tease,
They bring giggles with the breeze.

Bouncing high on blades of green,
They dance like you've never seen.
Each stumble leads to laughs galore,
As squirrels join the funny score.

Tickling flowers, swaying tall,
A merry band, they have a ball.
With every petal's joyful shake,
They share the fun that they awake.

As echoes ring through sunny skies,
You'll smile wide, you won't disguise.
In this place, where laughter flows,
The heart finds peace, and joy just grows.

Bright Smiles on the Breeze

In the meadow, laughter sprouts,
Every corner filled with shouts.
A cheeky wind pulls at my hat,
It's a game, and how 'bout that?

Butterflies, with wings so bright,
Join the fun, all taking flight.
Playing tag with giggly foes,
Nature chuckles, see how it shows.

The daisies shake, the daisies laugh,
As rabbits make a quirky path.
With each hop, a silly dance,
They prance about in pure romance.

Sun-kissed faces, wide and free,
In this moment, joy we see.
Among the blooms, a sweet release,
Let laughter grow and never cease.

Hearty Laughter in Bloom

With bursts of color all around,
In this patch of mirth, I'm bound.
Petals whisper jokes so light,
Each bloom twinkling with delight.

A hedgehog juggles apples small,
Stumbles, fumbles, but stands tall.
Fluffy clouds above look down,
Joining in the joyful crown.

Bees hum songs of pure delight,
Making rounds till fall of night.
While crickets play their harp so sweet,
We dance to rhythms in our feet.

Here among the flowers bright,
Laughter blooms and takes its flight.
In this space where joy ignites,
Every moment feels just right.

Delight in the Green Embrace

A patch of shade, a gentle laugh,
A playful pup, the perfect path.
Under trees where branches sway,
We find our hearts in light ballet.

With every rustle, secrets shared,
Nature's jesting, hearts laid bare.
Leaves giggle as the sun dips low,
In this realm, our spirits grow.

Squirrels chatter, playing tricks,
Among the twigs, with little licks.
Worms in wiggle, what a sight,
They join the fun, pure delight!

As shadows stretch and day takes flight,
We're wrapped in warmth, feeling just right.
In the green embrace, we roam free,
Where laughter thrives, just you and me.

Tickle of the Wind in the Grass

In the meadow, whispers play,
Breezes dance, and giggles sway.
Flowers nod with laughter bright,
As sunbeams chase the day to night.

Caterpillars wear silly hats,
Bees hum tunes like chitchat chats.
Clouds above do somersaults,
Nature's jest, it never halts.

A rabbit trips on his own feet,
While ants march on, feeling the beat.
Each blade of grass a ticklish friend,
Where silly moments never end.

In this green maze, jesters roam,
Creating a cheerful, laughing home.
Laughter echoes, pure delight,
In every frolic, day and night.

Carousel of Ecstasy in Nature

Round and round the flowers twirl,
Bees and butterflies swirl and whirl.
Sunshine showers warm embrace,
Joyful giggles we can't efface.

Squirrels scamper with a wink,
Over trees, they dash and blink.
Swinging high from branch to branch,
Nature's jesters take their chance.

Frogs croak tunes of silly cheer,
Jumping high, they persevere.
In the pond, with splashes wide,
Every ripple takes the ride.

Round they go, a puzzle bright,
Where every spin brings pure delight.
The carousel spins for all to see,
In nature's whimsy, wild and free.

Fanciful Frolics in the Field

Among the daisies, laughter rings,
Grasshoppers leap with playful flings.
Dandelions puff their fluffy dreams,
While nature bursts with giggly beams.

Puppies chase their tails around,
Every tumble makes a sound.
Butterflies flit in joyful dances,
While rabbits dodge with silly prances.

Mice in hats plot their surprise,
As giggles echo, twist and rise.
In every corner, fun unrolls,
Nature's secret, joy consoles.

Fields alive with vibrant cheer,
Where laughter bounces, drawing near.
In the frolics, life's a gift,
In every smile, our spirits lift.

Jubilant Whirl of the Wild

In the forest, branches sway,
Gentle creatures come to play.
Squirrels leap from tree to tree,
Chasing fun with joyful glee.

Wildflowers sway, a colorful sight,
Colors twinkle in soft daylight.
The breeze brings whispers, secrets shared,
As nature's chorus sings unprepared.

Near the brook, splashes fly,
Fishes leap to say goodbye.
All around, a joyous sound,
Where laughter in the wild is found.

With every rustle, playful calls,
The forest echoes, joy enthralls.
In this whirl, life dances bright,
Nature's jesters, taking flight.

Frolicsome Breezes

The wind plays tag with dandelions,
Tickling the toes of lounging lions.
Laughter spills in every nook,
As nature dances, come take a look.

Tiny bees in a buzzing race,
Flit through flowers with silly grace.
A squirrel slips, a tumble and roll,
Echoes of laughter in the living scroll.

Grass blades sway like giggling friends,
As sunlight shines and softly bends.
In this realm where fun is found,
Jubilant whispers swirl all around.

So come and join this merry cheer,
Where joy abounds throughout the year.
Let frolicsome breezes set you free,
In nature's jest, let your heart be glee.

Playful Shadows on the Lawn

Shadows stretch like silly cats,
Bouncing around like playful bats.
The sun decides to play a game,
With flickering light, it calls your name.

A picnic blanket, all spread wide,
Brings smiles and giggles, side by side.
Sandwiches dance, apples roll,
In this carefree, humorous stroll.

Kites soar high in the azure sky,
With colorful tails that wave and fly.
Each gust of wind brings hearty grins,
As laughter twirls and spins in winds.

With friends around, the fun won't cease,
Every moment's filled with sweet release.
So come to where the shadows play,
And let your worries float away.

Smiles in the Sunlit Glade

In the glade where sunbeams peek,
Little giggles rise and squeak.
Butterflies join the lively cheer,
As joy and laughter fill the sphere.

A rabbit hops, so full of glee,
Wiggling its nose, wild and free.
Chasing shadows, a curious dance,
Each leap brings forth a new chance.

Crisp apples drop with a funny thud,
Creating ripples in the grassful flood.
Nature's chorus sings a sweet tune,
While daisies sway beneath the moon.

In this sunny, vibrant space,
Every smile is adorned with grace.
So linger awhile, let happiness grow,
In smiles and sunshine, let joy overflow.

Whimsy in the Weeds

Among the weeds, a secret place,
Filled with laughter, dreams, and grace.
A ladybug donned in red, so bright,
Bobbles along in sheer delight.

The ants parade in a funny row,
Marching with a purpose, into the glow.
Each tiny step, like a joke well-told,
In the meadow's warmth, they all unfold.

Tickling grasses wave and sway,
Inviting all to come and play.
Laughter ripples through the air,
Whimsy reigns, without a care.

So venture forth to this joyous scene,
Where laughter dwells, and hearts convene.
In the weeds where fun runs deep,
Join the revelry—no need to peep.

Revelry on the Rolling Hills

Laughter dances on the breeze,
Chasing clouds with playful ease.
A tumble down the grassy knoll,
Where joy and mischief take their toll.

Bouncing sheep with fluffy coats,
Join the fun as laughter floats.
A picnic spreads with goodies rare,
Friendly faces everywhere.

The sun dips low, the shadows play,
As nature sings the close of day.
A giggle here, a snort over there,
Laughter echoes, fills the air.

Together we roll, we slap our knees,
And spin like tops around the trees.
With each wild jest, our spirits fly,
In this gleeful dance beneath the sky.

Lighthearted Moments by the Stream

A skip of stones, a spray of glee,
Reflections giggle, wild and free.
Wiggly worms in a slippery race,
Catch the chuckles, pace by pace.

Frogs leap high with a joyful croak,
Their playful antics, a grand old joke.
Splashing water, a pranky spree,
Is there ever too much laughter? Not for me!

Breezes carry whispers soft,
As daisies nod and rise aloft.
Tickling toes in the stream so cool,
Each ripple adds to the playful rule.

As daylight fades, glowworms shout,
In glowing hues, they flit about.
With every light, a smile ignites,
Laughter lingers through the nights.

Frolics Under the Oak Canopy

Under branches, shadows sway,
Beneath the leaves, we laugh and play.
Squirrels dance with acorn pride,
While tales of wonder echo wide.

A gentle breeze tickles our nose,
As silly stories in circle pose.
Fluttering wings make giggles rise,
Butterflies wink, oh what a surprise!

We climb and tumble on grassy beds,
With silly hats atop our heads.
An oak tree whispers secrets near,
While joy and laughter persevere.

As dusk approaches, we find our way,
Swaying like branches in disarray.
With whispered giggles, we bid adieu,
For the memory of laughter feels ever new.

Cheerful Tunes of the Tiny Creatures

In the meadow, songs take flight,
From crickets chirping, pure delight.
Beetles bump in a rhythmic dance,
While twinkling fireflies take the chance.

A chorus of frogs in playful tone,
Ribbit and croak, never alone.
In this symphony, heartstrings pluck,
With notes of joy, we're out of luck!

Each tiny critter has a part,
As nature creates an artful heart.
With playful spins and silly tricks,
The forest floor becomes the mix.

When night falls soft, the laughter grows,
In the silence, where fun still flows.
For every chuckle, each giggle small,
The tiny creatures bring joy to all.

Mirthful Melodies in the Breeze

The wind whispers secrets, a tickle and tease,
While daisies dance lightly, with flicks and with flees.
A squirrel finds acorns, and trips on a root,
He tumbles and chuckles, oh what a hoot!

The clouds wear their laughter, as they drift on high,
Painting silly faces, against the blue sky.
A butterfly winks, in the glow of the sun,
With each spirited flutter, it seems we all run!

Amidst buzzing bees, and the chirps of the lark,
A frog steals the show with a leap and a quark.
Nearby, all the blooms in a riotous cheer,
Join in with the laughter, come gather, come near!

So come spin and sway, where the joy finds its place,
In the mirthful embrace of this carefree space.
Let nature's sweet giggles, and chuckles take flight,
In shadows of sunlight, where laughter feels right.

Corners of Bliss in the Valley

In the heart of the valley, where chuckles abound,
A jolly old goat prances, all silly and round.
With capers and bleats, he jests to the trees,
Making waves of bright laughter float high on the breeze.

The flowers are whispering, sharing a joke,
While the brook giggles softly, with each playful stroke.
A rabbit wears spectacles, reading a tale,
And the punchline erupts from a nearby snail.

With every soft rustle, a giggle takes flight,
As the sun dips low, painting everything bright.
And shadows grow longer, but the fun's not yet done,
As crickets hold concerts, where all will soon run!

So gather your friends, let the merriment swell,
In corners of bliss, there's a story to tell.
With laughter that echoes, in echoes so sweet,
In the valley of fun, where the silly hearts meet.

Charm of the Cheerful Glade

In the glade of delight, where sunlight does play,
A mischievous hedgehog rolls round on his way.
He tumbles through clover, in giggles and spins,
Creating a ruckus, where happy begins.

The trees lean in closer, to hear all the fun,
As crickets and chirpers join in on the run.
A fox tells a story, with a wink and a grin,
And laughter erupts from the hearts, warm within.

The daisies are winking, under the bright sun,
In a playful debate, of who's fastest to run.
While butterflies flutter, in a swirling ballet,
Each moment a treasure, in this charm of a day!

So weave through the laughter, let your spirit soar,
Join the glade of the cheerful, you'll find so much more.
With nature as witness, and joy to bestow,
The charm of this glade, will forever bestow.

Dances of Delight in the Wilds

Where the wilds come alive, with a jump and a caper,
The critters engage in their dance with a paper!
Raccoons wear top hats, with a flourish so grand,
While owls hoot in rhythm, keeping time with a band.

A parade of bright fireflies flicker and sway,
Lighting up all the paths, in a whimsical play.
Chirping and chortling, the night air rings clear,
With every skittering sound, more friends gather near.

The twirls and the spins, of the creatures so spry,
Underneath the moonlight, where giggles don't die.
The bushes are shaking, with laughter and cheer,
As even the shadows decide to draw near!

So come join the party, let your spirit ignite,
In the dances of delight, where every heart's light.
With joy in abundance, let loose and be free,
In the wilds of enchantment, there's magic to see.

Brightened Spirits on the Path

Beneath the sun, the shadows play,
With giggles bouncing on the way.
A squirrel prances in a dance,
While flowers nod in a fleeting glance.

A hat blown high, a chase ensues,
With muddy shoes, we stomp and bruise.
The laughter echoes, crisp and clear,
A joyful song for all to hear.

In every step, a touch of cheer,
As butterflies draw ever near.
A feathered friend, so bold and spry,
Joins in the fun, as we all fly.

So take a breath, let spirits rise,
Beneath the blue and sunny skies.
With every laugh, each moment bright,
The world transforms, pure delight!

Delight in the Dew-Drenched Grass

Morning breaks with glistening jewels,
Tiny worlds where mischief rules.
A playful breeze, a tickling touch,
Invites the sun - oh, how we clutch!

Tiny footsteps on the green,
A sassy fox we have seen.
With paws that dart and tails that flip,
Oh, what a tangled, joyful trip!

Rolling headlong through the dew,
A giggle shared by me and you.
With every tumble, every fall,
We rise again, we take it all.

The grass beneath, our merry stage,
Unfolding laughter, we engage.
In every drop, a spark of fun,
The day goes on, we'll never run!

Carefree Chimes of Laughter

In fields alive with painted blooms,
The breeze whistles cheerful tunes.
Children chase the sunlight's glow,
While shadows dance and spirits flow.

A silly hat atop a tree,
With laughter ringing wild and free.
The clouds above join in the glee,
As dreams take shape in jubilee.

With clinks and clanks from games we find,
Each moment fresh, uniquely designed.
A wobbly bike and squeaky wheels,
Life's sweetest bliss, it brightly reveals.

So join the flock where joy takes flight,
As smiles and giggles feel just right.
A day of fun, we'll not forget,
In every heart, a cheerful debt!

Radiant Revelries of the Earth

Through whispered woods, adventures call,
On joyful rides, we break the fall.
Rumbling tummies, a picnic spread,
With laughter shared, and crumbs of bread.

An acorn drops, and laughter swells,
A scatter of giggles, the tale it tells.
Bouncing frisbees, and swirling skirts,
A planet of joy beneath our shirts.

The sun dips low, but spirits soar,
With fables spun from tales of yore.
Around the campfire, stories play,
As stars above greet the close of day.

We count the wishes as they fly,
With every twinkle in the sky.
In zestful hearts, the world expands,
Embracing laughter, hand in hand!

Frolics Among the Flora

In a patch of blooms so bright,
Bumblebees waltz in the light.
A butterfly trips on a petal,
Even the daisies start to giggle.

A squirrel twirls with a nut in hand,
The sun smiles over the land.
Ladybugs play tag on the vine,
Nature's jesters, oh how they shine!

The wind whispers secrets of cheer,
As rabbits hop, full of good cheer.
Jests echo from tree to tree,
This garden's a stage, wild and free.

With laughter stitched in every leaf,
The flowers sway in disbelief.
Tickled by breezes, they sway and spin,
In this vibrant world, we all win!

Serendipitous Snickers in the Grassy Nook

In the shade where the shadows play,
A toad sings in a quirky way.
Grasshoppers dance with nimble feet,
Their humor makes the day so sweet.

Crickets chirp in a merry choir,
As ants march on, without a tire.
The daisies bob in a joyful trance,
Inviting all to join the dance.

Sunlight dapples through the trees,
Tickling noses in the breeze.
A fox sneezes, a startled crow,
Laughter erupts at the silly show.

While petals sway, the world feels light,
In this nook, all hearts take flight.
A giggle born from nature's jest,
In every creature, joy is blessed!

Joy Dance in the Garden

In the garden where spirits soar,
Blooming laughter at every door.
A gopher grins as he digs in,
While tulips wiggle, wearing a grin.

The sunflowers twist in playful glee,
Their faces turning, oh so free.
A lizard leaps with a cheeky flair,
Every moment, joy fills the air.

Bouncing beans in a colorful row,
Chasing shadows, one, two, go!
A butterfly flops with too much zeal,
Entwined in mirth, oh what a reel!

Every bloom a story to tell,
Of laughter shared, of laughter well.
In this garden, silliness reigns,
Where every sweet smile breaks the chains!

Glee Spreading Like Wildflowers

In a meadow bursting with hues,
Laughter sparkles like morning dew.
Dandelions puff and tickle the breeze,
Spreading cheer with the greatest ease.

A bear makes a fuss over honey's taste,
While neighbors chuckle, never in haste.
Every blossom a friend to the sun,
Their giggles rising, a joy-filled run.

Wiggly worms twist in a game,
Nature's jesters, wild and untame.
As flowers sway in a curvy line,
The world giggles, feeling so fine.

With every rustle, the fun expands,
A ripple of joy across the lands.
In this wildflower spree so grand,
Happiness blooms, hand in hand!

Whispers of Joy Among the Ferns

In the shade where ferns do sway,
   Little critters dance and play.
   A squirrel tells a joke so sly,
   While butterflies just flutter by.

Laughter rustles through the leaves,
As sunlight weaves and softly cleaves.
   A robin sings of silly things,
   And the laughter that it brings.

The hidden beetle starts a show,
With tiny moves that steal the glow.
   A froggy croak adds to the cheer,
   As all the friends gather near.

Their giggles echo through the trees,
   A symphony upon the breeze.
   In this patch of verdant cheer,
   Joy is simple, bright, and clear.

Playful Spirits of the Prairie

Across the fields where daisies bloom,
Breezy whispers lift the gloom.
A playful calf kicks up some dust,
While baby bunnies hop with trust.

The wind it carries giggles sweet,
As everything begins to greet.
A wise old owl cracks a grin,
As the sunset calls everyone in.

Mice in lines do dance in time,
Their tiny moves a joyful rhyme.
And on a stalk, a ladybug,
Tells tales of games they all have dug.

In the midst of grassy waves,
The creatures play like silly knaves.
Every laugh, a tiny spark,
Lighting up the evening dark.

Echoes of Laughter at Dusk

The sun dips low, the shadows grow,
A cackle rings from high to low.
A raccoon juggling berries bright,
Brings out the giggles of the night.

A pair of owls wink and hoot,
As crickets play their funny flute.
A hedgehog rolls beneath the moon,
Spinning tales like a funny tune.

Buzzing bees hum round the bloom,
Where fireflies light up the gloom.
In every nook, a smile gleams,
As laughter threads through nature's dreams.

These echoes dance on soft, cool air,
Reminding all to shed their care.
With every chirp and merry tease,
The night is wrapped in joyful ease.

Amusement in the Wild Garden

In the garden, chaos reigns,
As bumblebees tease little drains.
With petals bright and smiles wide,
Nature's fun can't be denied.

A worm in shades of lime and pink,
Is cracking jokes while flowers wink.
A snail in shades of glistening green,
Zooms past, though it's rarely seen.

The playground grows with hops and bounds,
Where every laugh is nature's sounds.
A mouse ties knots in blades of grass,
As green frogs leap and warmly amass.

Every leaf, a frame for glee,
Where nature's spirits dance so free.
In this patch where joy will thrive,
Laughter blooms and feels alive.

www.ingramcontent.com/pod-product-compliance
Lightning Source LLC
Chambersburg PA
CBHW051636160426
43209CB00004B/676